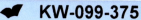
 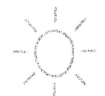 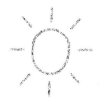

2

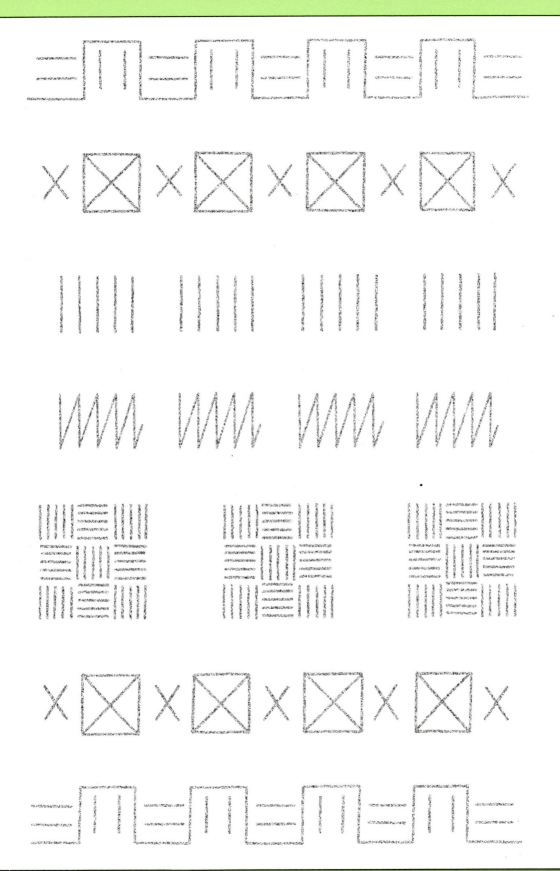

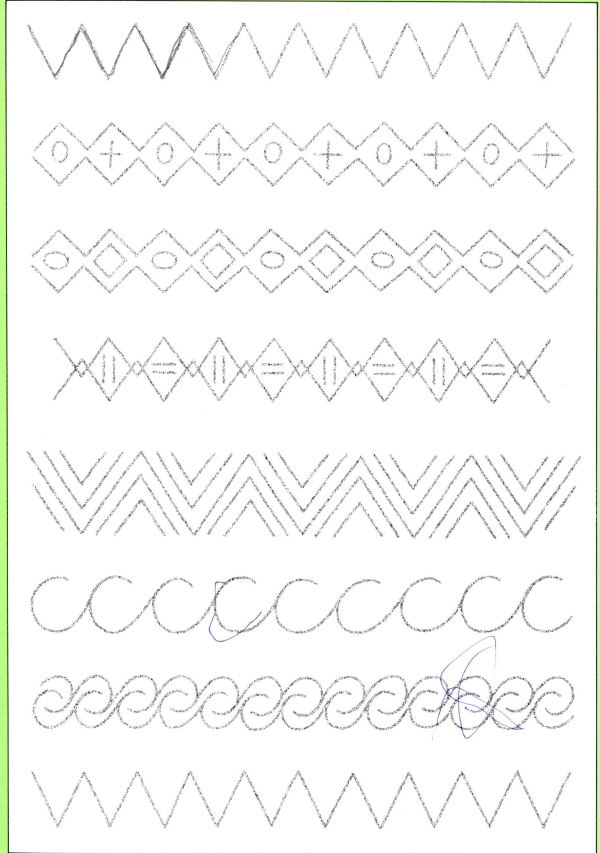

c c c   o o o   a a a

d d d   g g g   q q q

a c d g o q

good   dad   cage

i i i i   l l l l   t t t t

j j j j j   k k k k k

i j k l t

quick little jet

lllll uuuu mmmm

e e e e e s s s s s

f f f f f u u u u u

e f s u

stuff seeds fuss

b b b b b p p p p p

b b p p

baby paper pipe

mmmm ᐯᐯᐯᐯ mmmm

nn hh mm rr

h m n r

him her me man

v v v v w w w x x x

y y y y z z z z

v w x y z

wavy next lazy

VVVVVVVVVVVVVVVVVVVVVV

i i l l l   Iris   India

j j J   June   Japan

l l L L   Lucy   London

v v V   Victor   Victoria

w w W   William   Wales

z z Z   Zara   Zaire

ccccccc ccccccc

o o o o o o o o o o o o

c C Cinderella Cuba

g G Gary Germany

o O Oliver Oxford

s S Susan Sweden

u U Una Ulster

m M Mary Moscow

n N Nazreen Naples

t T Tom Turkey

x X X-ray Xmas

y Y Yvonne York

mmmmmmmmmmmmmmmmmmmmm

cccccccccccccccccccccc

nnnnnnnnnnnnnnnnnnnnn

b B   Betty   Belgium

d D   David   Denmark

p P   Peter   Poland

q Q   Quentin Quebec

r R   Ranjit Russia

mmmmmmmmmmmmmmmmmmmmm

cccccccccccccccccccccc

uuuuuuuuuuuuuuuuuuuuu

a A   Anne America

e E   Edward Egypt

f F   Fred France

h H   Helen Holland

k K   Kate Kenya

Relations

family   mother   mum

father   dad   brother

sister   son   daughter

relatives   uncle

aunt   cousin   niece

nephew   grandparents

grandma   granddad

The Alphabet

a A   g G

b B   h H

c C   i I

d D   j J

e E   k K

f F   l L

m M   t T
n N   u U
o O   v V
p P   w W
q Q   x X
r R   y Y
s S   z Z

Green Cross Code

First find a safe place to cross, then stop.

Stand on the pavement near the kerb.

Look all round for traffic and listen.

If traffic is coming let it pass. Look all round again. When there is no traffic near, walk straight across the road. Keep looking and listening for traffic while you cross.

Time

Sunday	second
Monday	minute
Tuesday	hour
Wednesday	day
Thursday	week
Friday	month
Saturday	year

Words for Maths

long   wide   high

length   width   height

weigh   balance

light   medium   heavy

number   few   many

enough   least   most

first   middle   last

Colours and Shapes

black   grey   purple

blue   orange   red

brown   mauve   white

green   pink   yellow

circle ⃝   rectangle ▭

square ☐   triangle △

oval ⬭   hexagon ⬡

Numbers

0 nought	7 seven
1 one	8 eight
2 two	9 nine
3 three	10 ten
4 four	11 eleven
5 five	12 twelve
6 six	100 hundred

Pairs

bat and ball

 bread and butter

cup and saucer

 fish and chips

king and queen

 knife and fork

table and chair

 # Animals

Pets   cat   kitten

dog   puppy   hamster

mouse   guinea pig

budgerigar   goldfish

Farm   horse   foal

sheep   lamb   cow   calf

hen   chicken   pig

 # Transport

vehicles   car   bus

coach   taxi   lorry

tank   tractor

bicycle   motorbike

scooter   train   tube

aeroplane   helicopter

ship   ferry   hovercraft

Seasons and Months

Spring   Summer

Autumn   Winter

January   February

March   April   May

June   July   August

September   October

November   December

The Countryside

cottage   farm   barn

fence   hedge   wall

meadow   field   grass

flowers   violet   daisy

barley   oats   wheat

ditch   stream   bridge

tree   wood   leaves

bird   nest   feather

Space

planet   sun   moon

star   world   earth

sky   horizon

rocket   shuttle

astronaut

gravity   oxygen

count - down

blast - off

People we Need

neighbours   friends

doctor   dentist   nurse

policeman   teacher

fireman   guard

driver   conductor

pilot shopkeeper miner

artist musician writer

soldier   sailor   airman

Food and Drink

cereals   bread   biscuits

cake   pudding

dairy produce   butter

cream   cheese   eggs

meat   bacon   chops

hamburger   sausage

vegetables   potatoes

beans   tomatoes   peas

Alphabetical Order

ant   bun   cat   dog

egg   fly   gun   hat

igloo   jam   kite

ladder   man   net

orange   pony   queen

rabbit   star   tent

umbrella   vase   water

x-ray   yacht   zebra

The Guppy

Whales have calves,

Cats have kittens,

Bears have cubs,

Bats have bittens,

Swans have cygnets,

Seals have puppies,

But guppies just have
little guppies.

Ogden Nash

I'm not Frightened of Pussy Cats

I'm not frightened
of Pussy Cats,
They only eat up
mice and rats.
But a Hippopotamus
Could eat the Lotofus.

Spike Milligan